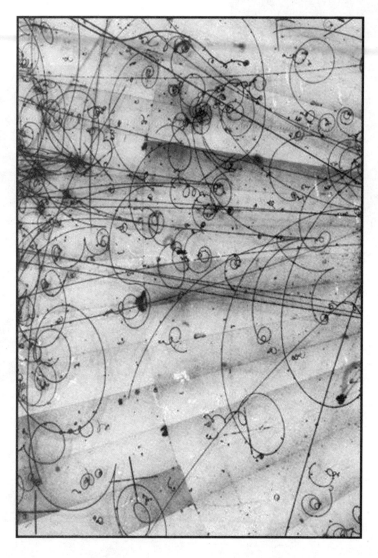

a blewointment book   2011   NIGHTWOOD EDITIONS

shane rhodes

err

Nightwood Editions
P.O. Box 1779
Gibsons, BC VON 1VO Canada
www.nightwoodeditions.com

TYPOGRAPHY & DESIGN: Carleton Wilson

Nightwood Editions acknowledges financial support from the Government of Canada
through the Canada Book Fund and the Canada Council for the Arts, and from the
Province of British Columbia through the British Columbia Arts Council and the Book
Publisher's Tax Credit.

This book has been produced on 100% post-consumer recycled, ancient-forest-free paper,
processed chlorine-free and printed with vegetable-based dyes.

Printed and bound in Canada

LIBRARY AND ARCHIVES CANADA CATALOGUING IN PUBLICATION

Rhodes, Shane, 1973–
Err / Shane Rhodes.

Poems.
"A blewointment book".
ISBN 978-0-88971-256-0

I. Title.

PS8585.H568E77 2011   C811'.6   C2011-900042-3

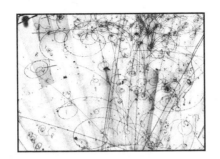

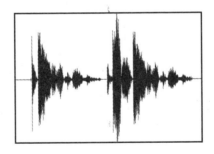

TABLE OF CONTENTS | *TABLE OF DISCONTENTS*

SPIRITS

BODIES

THE CLOUD CHAMBER

DARK MATTERS

SPIRITS

Et tu bois cet alcool brûlant comme ta vie
Ta vie que tu bois comme une eau-de-vie

Apollinaire

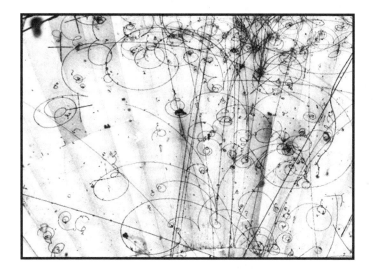

RISE SPIRITS,

Stagger up from caudled cups, fuddled sops
Revive & sway from allsorts pots, debauched sots
Crawl from bar stools & tabletops, soused gutter mops
From grain muck potato hunk grape must sugar lump
From warts washes & hops, you dipsomaniac drunks
From backdoor bathtub bootleg slapbang stillshops
From shady lounges bars & pubs
From ghostly palaces parlours ghostly dives & clubs
Come, whet your whistles tie one on & bever up
With a brew of purl sack hock pulque flip & junk
For you, tipsy tipple hogs & potationist punks
I tap the kegs barrels pipes & butts
I tip the flagons noggins flasks & jugs
For you, carousing lot, imbibe a damp a round a go
A shench a nug a squib a rub & a pint of hot
O, drink deep draughts of my wine dark plonk
Swill it swig it sling it toast it tope it toss it
O, glug gulp guzzle knock it back & lap it up
Now, as this firmament ferments for us, rise & slur
O, stumble up to orate & pontificate
From the faint fog, sway to ornate & obfuscate
Convivial mates, to oraculate & equivocate, o rise
Intoxicants, rise up & speak

Fucking drunk and erectly defunct, Tom Collins lies face down in the muck. Before Tom soured and bittered – before the tiny plastic sword, the B&B and the B&E – life was a strawberry daiquiri. But Tom, always over thin ice, soured and went ward eight for the hard stuff, public drinking, nightcaps and pubic dinking. Half-cocked between highballs and fuzzy navels, he'd suck back black Russians and slurp at old-fashioned pink ladies. Shake it/stir it – buy Tom a mickey and it didn't much matter. Flexible as a maraschino cherry stem, he'd spike his rusty nail on the cable car, muddle his mojito in the sidecar or drop a depth-charge on some wet bar. Come summertime, beneath a miniature umbrella, you could always find Tom with his piña colada shouting, *Woo woo!* during sex on the beach, such were the enthusiasms of his orgasms. Son of a boilermaker and a dirty bird, Tom's last Singapore sling was his Pearl Harbor. You can sometimes see him now in beer halls after eight boarding the red-eye with his mates: Rob Roy, Bloody Mary, Harvey Wallbanger.

1. *Harvest Notes*

> desire
>
> > > harvested late
> > crushed

2. *Vintner's Notes*

> The collected paperasse
> of faux sommeliers
> selected, malolacticly
> fermented to milk
> and strained
> through the white kid gloves
> of the late queen mum.
> Cellared in St. Vincent's
> hollow chest.
>
> Screw the rest.

3. *Serving Suggestions*

Serve with soft Yeti cheeses
or Ogopogo kabobs,
fillet of Loch Ness.
Try with Chimera compote flambé
in an essence of crude sauce
or the delicate smoked white meat
of Sasquatch pits
and Architeuthis calamari.

Pairs well with death.

4. *Tasting Notes*

Gooey globate gobsmacks
of jellied gingivitis
and jejune jujube juice
galloping gargantuan
in the gorge. Golly!
Guzzle it gingerly.
Guggle it like grub-gum
in a groaning Gregorian gargle,
both godly and goy,
or gloss over the garrigue
gewgaws with glee.
Generally, it's going to garrotte you,
grind and grunt.
Gently, the gastro-gibbet gimcracks
will gaff you,
gape and gag.

This grainy gunk,
a good gallows-glug,
is glum gossamer.
It's greasy grape-glut.
It's like gothic gouda gabbled
with glacial granite gravel.
It grabs you in the gutbucket
as a garish gardyloo
from the gloryhole.
Go get this generic jam
it's only a gazillion gold guineas
for grand gourmand gaga.
Give it as gift to your guy,
grant it as graft to your gal,
or in gregarious gemütlichkeit
to your gay girlfriends –
those gorgeous gads.
Gauche, gosh yes, but gone
with genial glam
from your gaping goblet.
Given your gallon is gonzo,
by gar you're gonna grieve
from your grotto in the gutter,
your gasping gulch.

Two fingers in a cup of cut crystal. Swirl it and the spirits draw nearer, dis membered, thirsty for their mouthful. Even the glass cries. Tears. What envelops the tongue is insolence. What fills the mouth are peb bles. Beneath the sound of a shovel cleav ing peat, remember. My father is bur ied there, caged in oak, wrapped in tobacco leaf and cedar. Spring water smears his eyes.

COCKTAILS: THE RED REVOLUTION

for Prince Edward Distillery

Ack! Ack! goes the gun attack.
Back! Back! yell the junkers
    high on arrack, pontac
        and Armenian Armagnac.

        Where Tsars scoffed caviar and zakuski,
    bubbled samovars and inbred nobility
            drank nantz and spoke of Germany,
    now Volgas of unwashed humanity
ransack cellars for French whiskey
    and Irish brandy.

    Riff-raff of the underclass!
Commanderette Smirnoff
        shouts from the Palace loft,
    Ambidextrous Marxist-Leninists
sociopathic socialists
           drinking to the proletariat
      while robbing them like idiots,
to you, I toast this Molotov
        may it blow you back to the Romanovs!

With a last bottle of 1847 Château de Calme,
    an uncorked cellar servant:
        Ah – this was the Tsar's favourite
          and, oh, how he would savour it
    full of tannin and foreign profit
    (in 1812 we finished Napoleon
then, stuffed in a bottle, the Tsar brought him back in!)

now, who's to serve it

        and who's to drink it?

Indecent and undecanted,

Bolsheviks and Mensheviks united

    only behind a Russian claret!

        I can't stand it –

I saw a butler drink (drink!) a 1910 muscat!

        Débouché: Rotchilde, Montleau et Larose.

Entkorkt: Rudesheimer, Markobrunner und Musse.

    Sacked: Tokay from Hungary, Prince Golitzin's Honey.

        Reds before Whites!?

    Whites before Reds?!

        What a viniferous mess!

he yanked the cork and guzzled it.

    The last of the binging barrel-chested Cossacks

    pours out a monologue:

War, money and hijacks!

    Brothers, Kerensky's split

and we are, for the moment,

    the new government.

The first bill I back

is this rare Georgian cognac

    filched from the Tsar's own caback.

    It smells of Siberian prison stocks

    and my sweaty socks

but, as I second it,

    my constitution grows elegiac.

Comrades, d'you know of the angels' share,

    stolen booze, taken by the air?

    It's like Russia, I fear, forever dreamt

but never there –

18

distilled by quacks
    labeled the New Aphrodisamnesiac
            and sold to another round
      of despotomaniacs.
            With a final vote, he raised his glass,
   this Assembly's closed
      and my bill is passed.

MURDER ON THE ROCKS

for PEI's Strait Shine

Up spirits! Alarum!
Muster drums & trumpets,
prepare tantrum's rostrum
for a dunder tumbler rumbler
& rummy variorum.
Take sweet saccharum
& distill lacrimae rerum
of Europe's delirium,
Guinea's erumny
& cimarrónes in irons.
Affront humdrum doldrums
with a raw rumbullion –
deftly draw the drumly
tap the taffy tots
& with a gill of grog
irrumate the nasty nostrum.
Oh, jorum of aurum –
Ad, sacred sailor serum –
Ah, conundrum's colostrum –
Ho, mare liberum in a rumkin –

Frumth indecorum
thrump Reina & royaume
screech brumled rumbellion!
Once galleons ran rhumbs,
now batty Bacardi barons
club Havana & rumba.
Fulcrum to Benin's bite
& coked Cuban lustrum –
on the tongue, an empire burns
in simulacrum.

> and moved by the demonstrable effect
> of great Art and the brotherhood of people I remarked
> "– the poem oughta be worth some beer"
> – Al Purdy, "At the Quinte Hotel"

~~100~~

for Ottawa's Hogsback Vintage Lager

Mounseer,
    mon phreer,
ne'er e'er sneer
    at the careers
of clareteer
    balladeers.
From beer
    to cheer,
privateers,
    they, bleary-eared seers,
traveers
    life's bumsteers.
Braveer
    an' ne'er jeer,
spilliteer,
    our sonateers
are sauteers.
    God'll skeer ya
or I'll gambeer ya
    with a reerey
dictioneer.

99

for Steam Whistle Brewery

Labour is the old complaint, cold is the other.
For thirty-six years, I've stared down dirt
to my father's land-locked eyes:
grit that grinds with the reek
of rock bits and life ends,
the oiled sheen of his pint-sized hands
day deep in the guts of diesel machines
for the flash of grain futures on TV screens
and the itch of augured seed.

> *Listen, son,*
> *work will break your back,*
> *muddle your mind*
> *and smelter your mettle*
> *while you empty the bank*
> *to put bread on the table.*
> *Death is the easiest harvest,*
> *the rest is market*
> *where governments sell us*
> *and buyers starve us.*

My fathers and mothers under the loam
hitched to a common harness.

Taurus-tossed Orion, night shift zookeep, staggers at the horizon's edge. Beneath his drunken stumble, a tomcat warms in house drafts at my back door tonight. Black-brindle off-chance, fed on scraps from Italian restaurants nearby, I don't think he'll see the end of this January heat sink. Winter, I can't wait to see you stabbed by the thermometer's red blade. But what is death in this empire of ice floes and populated Plutos where office-folk shuffle in minivans from hinterburbs to marketmall? Snow falls and drifts, ash from a work camp. Nebula-groined Orion, from the mythical to the mundane, the stars have fallen from your name – into this adenosine triphosphate net of intellect. And your cat has disappeared too, or is out here somewhere, pawing old felonies, frozen crap, what remains.

97

for Beaus Brewery

Purdy?

~~March~~ April ~~May~~ b<u>ee</u>r
bo<u>tt</u>les blo<u>ss</u>om ~~Bud!!~~ ~~Busch??~~
to a br<u>oo</u>ding
te<u>rr</u>oir. ~~ch haiku~~

COCKTAILS: IN THE BEGINNING

for Victoria Spirits Gin

> Inspir'd by Gin, I'm ready for the road;
> Cou'd shoot my man, or fire the King's abode.
> – from the *Gentleman's Magazine* (1751)

In smoky light, every night the bingo caller, Genevan Royal Bob, and my
    gilded dabber daubed a gin-

pidgin of card margins, free centres, clickety click, and doctor's orders. I
    friggin'

tell you she, my madam, was half-baked on jacky, crank, jiggin' *Strip me
    naked, stark naked* beggin'

for a gingery cougue of Mother's Ruin, a little Cuckold's Cumfort from
    King Theodore of Corsica, whose origin

I measured in yards, max, of tape. Bingo war and I was dabbing for a
    blackout and gave her a shove in the mouth. With a dinky doo,
    twenty-two, the loyal engine,

a shiv of lightning blue, she shoved that Deadly and Co. as if a sapphire
    carcinogin,

a real knock me down, and my virgin dauber fell. Such malengin, an
   oggin of grief, it makes my lanugin-

ous lady's eyes water even now. Yet the blower blew a thirty-two, I missed
   the square and Old Tom yelled, *Bingo!* through a scroggin

mouthful. The game was up – to his burgining win, we waxed cerebral
   tabougins and raised a glass of celebrated butter gin.

NEW WORLD REDS

Buenos Aires

Bankers taste terror
in a fine malbec
feasting at the Tortoni
on the tears
of stocks and money.
On Avenida de Mayo,
all the new steps
are built on old
tango standards
kept in the navy's
torture chambers
now rent by the hour.
Munching Evita's
composted arias,
earthworms sing of terroir,
while stoned angels,
slipcast in pigeon shit,
stir in chrysalides
of Third Reich
honed leather.
Invalid generals
order cream for piles
file errant vendetta
and breathe deeply
the stomach gases
of the rotting unmasses
buried beneath the monolith
at the Recoleta.

SHOOTERS

postcard poems from the Americas

1 Pisco

Lima cries for Spain.

Spain was a swan in its hands
with a rosy cloaca
and a cock that tasted
of bullmeat.

Lima cries for Spain.

2 Cachaça

In São Paulo,
a monarch's fears
are many.

Yet few could imagine
the statutory pain
of a marble face
eaten by acid rain.

3 Mezcal

Boys sell Chiclets
in Tenochtitlan.
Beneath the catholic church,
Aztec temples.
Beneath Aztec temples,
the savage lake.
A man pastes posters
for a salsa band
at the temple gates.
And your mother, too,
they have raped.

4 Bourbon

On pillows of Hampshire green,
its father's breast,
Washington weeps
Keep! Keep!

5 Seco

¡SILENCIO! EVERYTHING!
In the cantina,
Panama is drinking.

6 Rum

Every song Havana sings
is a prisoner's song
from El Morro
with a voice of ballast rum
and sand.

Havana has much to offer.
Havana has HIV infection.
Havana has a lovely complexion.
Havana offers much of what it has.
Havana has shingles.
Havana has crabs.
Havana has what Havana has.

7 Chicha

In La Paz, men whistle. Men bang bangers and crank crankers. They thump and bump. They rub and hump. They harrumph. When the men speak, they speak only to say, *We men speak very little*. Men under their hair handle nuts and bolts like the breasts of women. They twist clockwise and counter-clockwise fitting things together. Men tighten things up. Men loosen things off. Men work at women with their hydraulic couplings. You can see men under pressure, beating within the heads of men. You can see men in their heads beating men. The soft skulls of men. The soft slick skulls of men. They could embrace men. They could kill men. Men hold gears to their teeth like apples or the beautiful tips of cocks. It is hard to take men, there are so many. Look at these streets in La Paz – covered with men.

8 Pisco

A massive steel beam is moved by a crane stencilled with the capital letters IOTA.

A man crouched on his haunches paints a chain-link fence with rust-coloured paint.

A woman rinses her mouth with water carried in pipes of copper mined from the open pits of Chuquicamata.

In the smoke from smelter #8, Maria and Co. incorporate.

At a meeting of the syndicata, a Codelco man raises his hand feeling a sudden secondary syphilitic stigmata.

He seconds the pain of Santiago.

COCKTAILS: THE MARTINI

an opera buffa

Of a mafia re, sing I.
Drawn by 400 prancing ponies
and four winged Pirellis,
he descends in a Maserati,
a big guy of the virtuosi
you can see his salami sway
like some reverse Salome.
His floozy is Mimi –
raised in Miami
but tanned in Waikiki
(sans bikini)
clad in knee-highs
and the pricey nihilis
of cultural amputees:
Versace, Armani,
Gucci and Missoni.
In the café, he shouts, *Bravi!*
and decrees Campari,
toasts his favourite jockey,
downs two Kamikazes,
a mai tai, a shot of rye,
and drops two tabs of ecstasy.
Holy moly, he liked a party!
Hoey! he yells to Mimi
yet, beneath the alcoholic ennui,
Mimi laps only Pelligrini
and eats hoity-toity antipasti.
As the room begins to sway,

five young Yamaguchi in khaki
armed with Israeli Uzis
spray high impact putti
willy-nilly
into the wounded feng shui.
Dropped kimchi
graffitis his Armani
and shakes his last dry martini:
gin, blood, Martini & Rossi.
Like Mussolini in Montessori,
the party turns topsy-turvy:
people go motley
recite Dante,
attorneys bray like donkeys.
The fait accompli
with a side of corpus delicti:
death sashimi (w/o wasabi)
– a fiat of someone's lackey,
a rich Russki in status nascendi,
or a Mata Hari GI
of the misanthropic miserati
spurned by love abandonné,
penis envy or plain greedy.
Dripping Pelligrini, Mimi:
Call off the Carabinieri.
In Little Italy, the modus operandi
is not the MI5 or the FBI.
Convey the rabbis and abbeys.
Sound it from the belfries.
An aria, she cries,
He was a bully, a Gemini
twinned to the vox populi

like a ventriloquist to his dummy.
He deserves no mercy.
Subterranean his industry,
he lived a quasi-Medici
beneath a Pompeii of money.
This calamari held high,
she brushes off the Italian parsley,
is his savoury memento mori
in a Mediterranean aïoli. She sighs,
Man drinks, therefore he dies,
and lays a gold card on his eyes.

CHOREOGRAPHED ECHOES

for Nicolas Théodore de Saussure

OH C_2H_5OH (aka alcOHol), alOHa!
HOwdy HÔte HOrnswoggle,
psycHO HOmocidal hellHOney,
cHOice of incOHerent HOmbres
adHOc cacopHOny
& melancHOlic HOoters
of barHOpping barypHOny.
as HOmopHObic pHOnophiles
cHOke on phallopHOric aphtHOngs,
bOHunk ooncHOoks
cHOmp OscHeal allopHOnes.
mucHO HOmo sapien bonHOmie.
abHOrring a macHO HOmme's
lecHerOus neurOHumour
(eg nOaH's nympHO-HOloury),
like a HOodlum's apHOtic arseHOle,
jeHOvahs, elOHims & mOHammeds
(ie HOly autopHObes in apHOny)
cHOir catHOlic prOHibitions.
yet etHanOl's eupHOria wHObbles
in icHOric brewHOuse batHOs:
paroopHOronic maHOOHoos HOg sHOchu,
gaucHO yaHOos sHOot samsHOo,
hip-HOppers HOard HOOcHinoo
bacHelOrs stOmacH scOtcH.
rHOdes' pantHOdic poetOmacHia
cHOrtles pletHOra (HOoray!),
fatHOms psycHOsis (boOHoo!),

ancHOrs cirrHOsis (bOtcHed HOrror!),
& autHOrs scHOlarly sympHOnic
biOcHem-HOkku.

> There is no greater enemy to Canada's material interests abroad this day than the
> wasteful, ruinous Drink Traffic. But while it overturns the home of plenty, it more
> cruelly still shatters the goblet of human happiness.
> – *The Canadian Temperance Manual and Prohibitionists' Handbook, 1884*

the eye sees the cock, the bottle, the blind pig, the cow, the snuffers, the
swan with two necks, the Greenland tiger and, then, in the corner, the
bishop's finger

the loosened lips – where bang-up palabras palpate the beer-bombarded
babber lips to a bebumped bebop of papaphobic Presbyteers proselyt-
izing the poor pourboire plebs and philobiblic pogey bait pandybatted by
bagpipes and baptist preacher pap – speak easy

the tongue sets up still in Whiskey Gap, Alberta and greatly diminishes
the industry of his majesty's subjects

the stomach, drafting the dominion's constitution at the Quebec Con-
ference in 1864, succumbs to the blasting influence of the sin-inspired
draught and vomits in a potted plant in Lady Monck's drawing room

the hands pad their resumé with devil's work – look busy

the fingers reach out to the blanched and branded members of this sad
host of hope-blighted creatures

the liver (its daughters are nervous and hysterical, its sons are weak, wayward, eccentric and insane), bare-chested, syphilitic and enfeebled by geneva, a naked child tugging at dry dugs, pauses between poses for the woodcut

the blood – addled, banjaxed, coguyed, dagg'd, cock-eyed, fuzl'd, groat-able, hammered, inebriated, jagg'd, het the kettle, laugered, moon-eyed, nimptopsical, oxycrocium, contending with the Pharaoh, quarrelsome, rudderless with all sails out, tavern-tokened, undertaken, Virginia fenced, waterlogged, xed, yanked and zombied – has, by all degrees, to like, approved, and immoderately drank thereof

the bile, running rum from Saint-Pierre to the American rum line, names its schooner I'm Alone

the heart, as penitence for the body's excesses, sends a five-dollar donation to the Independent Order of Rechibites and Father Kyran Walsh's Total Abstinence Band in St. John's, Newfoundland

FINAL CALL

for The Manx

It's spooky how far, that night, we pushed the dram
and how quick we pulled it from the publican's
hand. Muddled from three gin tonics, I saw La Fée Verte
and a leprechaun breakdance about the rim.
Halfway through a Jägerbomb, I met a Windigo
talking Hubble astrophysics to a Djinn.
Near the bottom of the jeroboam, was it Rimbaud
buggering Verlaine and toasting absinthe to Baudelaire?
Someone slurred in translated text, *U look green,*
your I's are red. With a blue Curaçao,
his mouth went O – it was surreal.
To blast beyond that Rubicon, I packed my engines
with tarry hash, swallowed a mouthful of the shroom
and spoke in tongues sidereal. The stars replied
in helium and hummed *Om Mani Padme Hum.*
The ballast cut, my spirit left the room.
From far below, some Buddha toned, *It's closing time –*
enlightenment is fluorescent, which my mind paraphrased
to that babble that bubbles from the Helicon
effervescent. Then he cracked the gates between
my eyes with a kiss of dehydrogenase.

BODIES

for J. T.

for M. L., RN

for D. B.

for M. L.

Pearl with its "ear" and two dangling lobes named for pears or hams the shape of them worn about a woman's wrist. It's like that, the stalled movement in Vermeer's painting of the woman with the pearl necklace – she holds the pearls up to the mirror (glass melted, hammered and cooled in Nürnberg) as if two luxuries compared. But the pearls, so white, reflected in oil paint, must have been fakes, konterfei, made in France with varnished glass or beads filled with fish scales and wax. Like white skin over wounds. Like where her mother burnt her with a lit cigarette – four in the back, two on each arm and nipple so the nipples, though hard beneath the touch, felt nothing. Her eyes rolling back into her head until only the white remains, mother-of-pearl-like sclera. And, with images like this, I'd love to turn to something one could paint but her mother must have smiled at the smell (tobacco, light down of hair, a quarter inch of skin) of burning a hole through her daughter. Like the pearls gathered by hand in the 1600s from the waters off Isla Margarita. The Guaiqueríes – henequen ropes tied to their feet – dove deep beneath the pounding sea until their lungs bled a frothy pink or they were taken by the whitetips that prowled the reef. This is its centre, that anything, looked at hard enough, bleeds history. The water churns red in a rising cumulus of torn meat. Sea dogs. We don't care. Only Bartolomé de las Casas cared and the frigate birds hung in black crosses high above the breaking surf. Like a map, you could track slave ships by the bodies left in their wake, he told the Spanish king. The canvas was rolled to look like a stalagmite and stored in a salt mine to protect it from the Allies or Nazis, I can't remember which. On her body, I would trace with my fingertip the path from wound to wound, as from one memory to another. Here, I remember how, every weekend during the month we met, an old German woman from Gaspé would arrive at the outdoor market with oysters, smoked eel, smelt, sprats. Fish scales sequined her dress. We'd buy oysters for a dollar each, twisted and crusted in calciferous muck that I'd push and prod with a knife feeling for that seal in the gunk. Opened, glossy, with an opaque edge of semen white, but, on the tongue, a wave of salt, shell and grit. Here, I remember how, when I was a kid, we bought bags of crushed oyster shells for our chickens so they could make the shells that sphered the eggs we'd eat. Wave upon wave. Circles within circles. My mother called to tell me that she, this woman who had been my lover, was dead – she'd read it in the paper. Suicide? AIDS? An overdose? She didn't know which but was proud to be the first to bring me such misery. Like a poem, Ponge said of oysters, so hard to open, blows mark the envelope.

THE COCKTAIL

for Donnie Peters (1964–1999)

          Donnie, we counted the days
till your death
      by tulip spears and lily bayonets.
              I last saw you in a has-been
        coat – fox fur – always a scene –
on 17th Ave. in November.
      Your bare feet in pumps
              breath aerosol with alcohol and smoke.
        Kiss me my blue-balled cowboy
my boy toy
    my call boy.
             Wasn't AIDS fucked your head
        but ten years of coke.

If you read poetry (you didn't)
      you might know Lorca (you wouldn't)
           rode a horse of pearl –
      a horse rode hard
and put away wet.
      His took less time than yours
           but obeyed all the rules
        of faggot death – here's the rhyme –
a gun blew the maricón rojo
      all over the avenue.

           Donnie, my disease Argonaut
        fleecing the golden pubes
my barber of the uncivil

my resurrected stiff
drag drags on
even amongst the dead.
So I want you as you weren't
not your second coming
a protease tease
in a 90-pound
negligee of sweat
and black sarcoma lace –
so late 1980s.
Lypo, pills, tubes, the shits
is it a eulogy
if we wished you death?

INTRAVENUS

Lynne, we met the day Don asked to suck me off
– not my cock, he made clear, but toes, without socks
[boys in sandals got him off] – you wheel through that memory,
your legs in casts, [the virus rhyming RNA
to [reverse transcriptase] your DNA]
bones sapped [Combivir, Saquinavir, Ritonavir] by the daily
pharmablasts to make you gag and keep the docs away.
Those were the days we worked in then:
homeless guys down on 2nd drunk on Old Stock beer by 10,
sex workers [hookers] dazed by night work
up from the streets for the free lipstick
and condoms [safes] we dispensed, high on heroin [smack],
or [as the cell becomes a sieve] coke [crack],
eyes blue with [another negative test] mascara or black
from pimp beatings in the parking lot [turns positive] out back.
Lynne, you fundraised, you spoke, you organized,
you were one of the few who could help men die
and I never once saw you, like me, teary-eyed.
Every day since then [this, the line I tend], I
see it, think it, caught [daring words to mean]
by habit [everything I've touched and seen]
my fingers still type its name [all caps]: "it"
that floating thing [Sex = Silence = Death] called a referent
as in *The doc says I've got **IT*** – voice quiver bold italics
carrying us away from the linguistic
things we never wanted meant: GRID, the gay plague,
the empty cipher AIDS and Christian placards saying *God Loves Fags*
[Insert thread: deadbody: *doc, i'm 21*
& just found out ive got HIV – i'm done]

Dead. I write it now between the faces
of the faceless
men who came and went [Figure 1: see this micron pic
of a lymphocyte swarmed by neon pink
viral replicants, look how they shimmer and dance – a sequin dress
of nothingness] like so many torn couplets
each with something new to mend.
Lynne, we were the same age but you got fucked
[the body with sex is blessed] and I didn't,
that's where our stories split – fucked
by a boyfriend who didn't know he had it,
fucked by the used needle he shot with, the pusher who pushed it,
fucked [it's also never at rest] by the grower
who grew it, the mule who shoved it up his ass at the border
and got through it, fucked [and can churn for years] by their needles
and plastic, the politicians with their votes
and budgets, and fucked [in its own blood] by the poster saying
He [a woman carrying a boychild] *Was An Innocent Victim* meaning
everyone else [and tears] deserved it.
You got fucked by [the infinite] a virus [and its 33,000,000 faces]
that loves everything it erases.
Lynne, so many words [you and the drugs got better] to say it,
why [we slept together in your bed] I haven't looked
for you since then, [no stupid rhymes] scared
of knocking you from that past [the living with the dead]
tense where [your bones began to mend]
a whole new life [no one screamed when you bled] was inserted in.

Treat your plumber's helper gently and keep him out of sun.

Practise putting on a pullover while manning the cockpit on your own.

You never know when jack will strike the jackpot so carry a rainjacket at all times. This is not "zipper morals" but a responsible way to get one's chimney swept.

Open the envelope carefully to avoid damaging your diving suit. Then, gently pull the cassock over the bishop's mitre.

If you plan to lap southern seas, do so over a half-cut nightcap.

As an alternative, before heading to the bush with a sleeping bag, why not try using your quail pipe to roll the tent over the tent peg?

If you have venetian blinds, pull them back so the Cyclops is deadeye in the Trojan.

The thingamabob should not cover the thingummies!

If you plan to do some uphill gardening, use lots of jelly on your hoe handle – you don't want the seed sack to split when carrying wild oats!

If your exclamation point becomes a dangling modifier, the head gasket might slip from the dipstick – this is the biggest single cause of gene pool failure. If it does this while varnishing the pole, obviously, stop the train! You will need a new hubcap before you get ball bearing grease everywhere.

If making sandwiches or moving from a mustard jar to a honey pot, never use the same Freudian slip twice.

Also, Freudian slips come in many textures and sizes.

Once you have sent your troops to the hinterlands, carefully withdraw and pull off your armor. Watch out, it will be full of live ammunition!

Remember: For trips to the Pink Palace in the Black Forest, rubber boots are essential. Riding stallions? Saddle up!

THE BODY

a recombinant documentary poem

so doc what do I do?
every time my fear of getting aids
is so intense
(too much soul pain)
iam a 25yr old guy
(from a very small town
and moved to the city for a better gay life)
gave fellatio to a Thai lady boy
(i had my curiosity, i aint gonna lie)
we met through web chatting
hand jobs in the cafeteria
her mouth in the theatre
(last 1 minute, ejaculation
swallowed immediately)
I believe the fear of AIDS
is remorse when sex is bad
(trans , girl that I dont like
and that is not very serious.)
I would like an advice from you
on how to manage death :
Is it acceptable to be with trans girl
that he does not like?
I kissed her sucked there nipples
Could this be late conversion?
blow jobs with lots of tongue
i purchased a lot of condom,
when you go to france
you gonna need em!!

i met with lot of girls
(thank you!!!)
this guy i shared bleached needles with
hiv+, i am worried this guy
i can't eat or drink
I realise I'm a late converter
god, i don't have much time
i need to know if you think this case?
I was at a strip club and the stripper tongued my ear –
is this HIV?
1 in 1,000? 10,000? 100,000?
listen I am totally fuc
i might actually kill myself
I have a friend, 35,
bottomed his way to the top
(los CD4 eran 620 y la CV indetectable)
b/f cheated with a trisexual
the girl he was killed herself
because her husband had aids
He said he had been being tested
butt he condom broke
lol
there might have been pre cum,
I can't say there wasn't pre cum
could there have been precum?
should i start talking pep?
ive always known I was positive
(it must be a rare strain)
i have no desire
for a med filled life with sides
Is my whole life pre cum?
lol

.please save me
Now i want to make sex with wife
shall i wear that latex garbage condom?
52 year old woman in menopause
she is a slut or i dunno
but god i love this girl
unusual vaginal discharge
(five years in that army)
unprotected anal
(antigenic shift and drift)
lubed with spit it hurt so bad
i had blood
and sucked his nipples
(I am pretty
sure there wa snom ilk)
I just need to know if 1.
Was the protracted bj and nipple sucking
even worth it?
would HIV survive a lollipop?
book? brother in law?
(cuz the virus is all over the place
but gets active when it gets into an orgasm)
God, I'm only fifteen and I don't want something like that!
i swallowed my own sperm
and its quite many!!
PLS help me!!!
If a guy give another guy oral
(everyone cums in his mouth)
does he can still live healthy forever
& live happily ever after with me?
i love him so much! very2 much!!!
I parked my car

shat myself
I cried
shat myself
mon chere docteur, j'ai tellement besoin
shit?
I guess I'm reching out tonight
I guess I find my strength
and meds
within
I guess i wanna know
whos neg whos poz
when every ache, every cough
is the virus taking away
whats fake
I mean, I knew it was the HIV
killing me slowly
softly
you see, i'd been neg 23 times
when he raped me
and ejaculated inside me
and youre the first person I'm shearing this with
Hello, I can't pay for one of my meds this month
Hello, I've become resistant
Hello, I'm using a vibrator in the shape of a pussy
with an open sore on top of my virginia
we did it in my backside
(illegal in North Carolina)
I licked her clit vigorously
barebacked three tops
(fucked by man with Jesus tattoo pero
no hubo eyaculación interna ni sangramiento)
and wonder if that makes the odds more even?

you see, we lost our baby
and he wants to have another
(viral load over 10 million)
but I won't make it –
so doc what do I do?

amorous
an us
between us
bicurious
biflorus
chorus
coitus
cunnilingus
decubitus
ejectitious
erogenous
fabulous
gorgeous
hortus
humanus
Icarus
in us
Jesus
kindly adulterous
lickerous
locus
mucus
nexus
on us
phallus
Priapus
quietus
raptus
rictus

sanctus
secretous
stimulus
through us
under us
Venus
virus
with us

THE CLOUD
CHAMBER

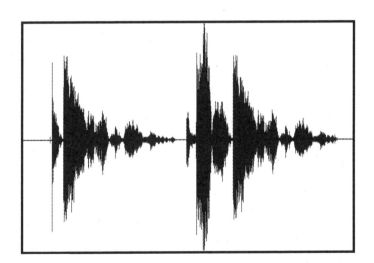

FOOL'S GOLD

X. Right there. Exactly. Our ambosexual
extispex prodded the viscera
and, on the vellum, X-ed a line
at a four-star crux.
Exclaiming *Abraxas!*, I expect
s/he was looking for extra, a tip

or a sign – her eyes dripped wax, his ears
were crossed. We fixed the course
and the pyxis spun as we set sail
for fabled Xanthoxin –
an all-expense annex
just south of Xanadu. Across axis

X, passing the Ancient Mariner
on his new SeaDoo, like pirate flix
with cheap FX, no kraken exploded
from no Styx. Extras wandered the ship,
eyes X-ed out like the dead in comix.
All in all, our luck was mixed.

Then the vespers relaxed to a voiceless velar
and we spotted it in the convex:
the island, the floating X.
We hugged and expressed
miniature "x"s of our feelings –
it was complex,

like MDMA or cybersex.
We excavated the augured site
as the cameras examined our excitement,
prime time, extracting boxes
of faux onyx, hoax zeuxite
and fXXXing pyrite.

ARABIAN LIGHT CRUDE

Golden is the voiceless fricative
yet, when angels sing, you can hear the price of gasoline.
Shh, shushed the Saudi sheikh, shielding his eyes
from the desert sun as, into the Aramco ship,
the last spout drops dripped
like the final notes from a shawm.

Cerebrally, he strums the crude homocline
beneath the Shahanshah's figuline eardrum.
Shhh. You can almost sense it:
first the shahnai, then the shakuhachi,
then the sheng – each reed hum
a shadow of the essence, the spirit,
the high-octane one.

He stretches his sandals through the poly shag
and sings – like a sibyl, like a shaman –
the siffling song of the sandy Shaybah
as, *shhhh,* his shaheen shits
on the sleeve of his thawb.

On the chinook, the shamal –
a shrill figurine, she flew
beneath the shewel
of drill strings,
legs shackled by jewels
of benzene.

PICK A WINNER

As God's my caller,
who locks money on a tongue-tied mudder
when the odds-on favour a free-legged pacer?
At the spit box, I run my hand
over the sulky tack of a ridgling geld –
the pin-hooker's false favourite.
I remember my first, my maiden break,
putting my father's fifty on a bay that placed
– his fists of cash, his sandbagged face.
Now, I wonder IfandOnlyIf has the conditions right
against IfNWhen? Do two maybes make a might?
Nothing's so sure it can't be chalked
on the midfield tote – what chance
I'll sock my bookie on the nose? 10 to 1
if I'm a little tight? In the sixth, a rabbit
fattens the pace for a wind-sucking entrymate
while my also-ran fails to place –
I'm not talking nose or head but ten fucking lengths!
I take a fifth of rye in the eighth
and lay two large on a chestnut filly
and, on a girl by the bar, a vodka martini.
But she wants a winner not a tout
and spits the bit on her garden trip.
Scratched. No blanket finish. Locked out.

THE SWITCH

Engine to mouth agurgle, he chugs
as his mother mans the spoontrain
charging steam (*Choo! Choo!*)
on a quid of chow. A beat unpitched?
A pro quo itched? What means
palato-alveolar affricate? Below?
Underneath? Uh huh, sandwiched
between his cowcatch teeth,
the platform for his first foul words:
Son of a bitch, obscene little fucker,
chomp soap and listen to your mother.
Her voice chugs and dopples
down memory's long traintunnel
mulched and gnawed by retched glottal stops.
But that train chuckled from the station
years ago, the child's grown up,
chums trucks in charcoal britches,
checks dials, chuffs his cap
and chortles whistles heard afar.
Which derailed my thoughts of lunch
with echoed chords of upchucked chop
and change on tracks crushed by trains –
the two-bit queen, what a chump,
every chance she took it on the maw.

METHOUGHT

Lost near the loughs nigh Loughborough
I saw naught but my airy thoughts
in a fog so rough it choughed the throat
and poured in the lungs like draught.
My lot: up to my houghs in naught, naught
but a slough in the bog, nothing land
towns like Loughborough slough off
where I mind no ghosts but those I ought,
the knightly slaughter forefathers and daughters
fought. Now, the unploughed troughs,
fraught by drought, planted with never a thought
but that bit of kneading haught the rich slough off –
dough for all the sought things that can be bought.
Though not by us – toughs and borough dogs
(*Bough wough! Bough wough!* hear us cough
like our throats will never be clear enough)
worth barely a laugh – so tightly wrought,
so thoroughly lost. Lost like I'm lost,
caught between "through" and "thought"
in the soughing soughs and the cloughing bloughs
where oughing English goes to rot.

F is frayful friction, like the fighter jet F-16
while two fingers (V) fake the fiction of peace or victory.
With gruff fs, the fox huntsman tallyhos his lazy dogs
lost in Mickey Finns and GHB, high on soporific fogs
while the four-foot vamp in vetch
flits her tail and flees – she fights for a land unfetched.
Over cliff and bluff, the huntsman flings his arsenal
of frag grenades, Tomahawks and UAV extraterrestrial
drones to steeplechase the vixen terrorist
with a palindromic xylophone. Forest informants
waterboarded say the bitch is Archduke Ferdinand
or a UVF defender of the Red Paw-Hand,
while fomenting counter-spooks rumour WMD
and an IRA sleeper cell, pet name Synecdoche.
Vermin of herded love, the well-versed floozy jumps:
she scuffles in living furs and muffs, she tussles in velvet fisticuffs.
On fenland tongue or covert lip, she leaves the huntsman forfeit –
he fuffs his horn, his hounds hold fast
till the vapid mastiffs pick up again the inky
scent: the beagles turn, the pointers point at me.

WITH GREAT THREAT, GREAT THARF

Let there, quoth she, *be dental fricatives*
on bent knees, *and light tithing.*
Throw in some "therefores," those "begats,"
and that's that – print it.
She, theological thane
of the cloth and spouter
of thick theandric theorems.
Like a thespian on a theologium,
she played her sermons like a theremin,
enthralled and eerie.

Before the apple and sloth,
consonants murmured,
vocoids fluttered.
Then, from the apex
of that naked tongue tower,
tearing larynx from pharynx,
throat from mouth,
He threw sound down.

Now?

The tongue twists
to tooth-tossed lippy jibber-jabber
as whutherred huther-muthers
thrash it with kathak yackety-yak.
Even the thester thalam
froths as throaty jaw-jaw
threatens porny patha-patha.

Absurd she thought it. Dumb. Unsound.
Thwart them, she obtested,
thou thegosistic thwacker,
let thy sky threaten thunder.
Forsooth them, she impetrated,
uproot the tongue,
flood the fauces,
cleanse this earthly palate.

·

THE HORROR

Umpah! Umpah! our tuba-wallah
hammered polkas while, on our howdah,
our hooters hooted, *Hooshtah! Hooshtah!*
Like hothouse rajas on pharma-safari
in African savannahs (our howlers
howled, *Hurroosh! Hurroosh!*),
for high tea we hookahed the holy herb
and hot knifed hash
on a haberdashed hibachi.

Expat pooh-bahs. Bohemian Brahmans.
HRH's hemispherical goombahs.
We drank stengahs as pariah lackeys
in purdah hovered with punkahs.

Hungry? We hoovered huevos
and exotic hoosh (*Hip hip!*),
tabbouleh, hummus, lahars of rahat lokum (*Hip hip!*),
and bahars of homey hominy (*Hurrah!*).

Money? *Pshaw!* We heaped hogsheads
with heaps of futah, gurrah and sannah.
We haggled (*No baksheesh!*) export pitarahs
of Hawaiian hula hoops, Honduran huaraches,
and Haitian cheetah-skinned doodahs.

Housed in a hebe-hobbledehoyhood
of nanas and ayahs, from hammocks
we hollered, *Heaven! Hell!* at the heathens
as, horny, we hammered their harems
and whooped, *The whores! The whores!*
in high holy hallelujah.

TSURIOTOSHI

Asashōryū Akinori,
yokozuna, Ulaanbaatary,
sways with his sagari
and eyes weighty Kyokushūzan.

To his yang, he was yin:
    to his ylang, he was ylang.

Since only yob-boy Makushitas,
yary early in the heya
they'd buoy heavy sacks (such yakka),
and salty yaffles for steamy yabbas
of chankonabe and yardas of yeasty sake.
They'd shiko (*Yam! Yam!* went their tummies)
until flabby bellies ached and borborygmied
like yeti yodels in the Alps.

Back in the dohyō
in a double yoke of arms
like two yaboos yarned in a yogi's yantra,
yawf for yawf the rikishi yandied
trading yips and yelps,
yarms and yamphs,
they yang-koed yet neither yielded.

Yak fucker, Akiniori yakked in Yakut.
Shut your yawp, Batbayar yapped.

Finally, like some spunky Yoshiwara,
Akinori yanked Kyokushūzan's hairy mage
(*Yarooh!* he yelled)
and the collected yabs of sumo yawned.
Was that his Kimarite? the yokels yattered.
Did he just yowf his you-know-what? they yabbered.
The gyōji yaffed, *You're no yakuza and he's no flunky!*
For fighting grubby, you get hansoku-make!

From such injury, rose Kyokushūzan's last kinboshi.

SINUOSITIES

Spelunking in the upper ethmoid, looking
for a gangling beast, the Pterygopalatine Ganglion, gurgling
nasal goo and wheezing snot. Talking
on my 4G, Singapore rang saying
Go hang – we're selling no more of the fake Ming
sake servers you're making with the chain gangs of Sing Sing
– in the big house by day banging
rocks, by night, hungry, they clung
to such bling, pfennigs each in Geising.
From the grungy depths, going
further, we heard mangy Maxilla, clanging
amongst sinus chambers, groaning
like a dangerous jungle-thing.
Air sampling, we were finding
traces of dung, bong gunk and ginseng
like an arranged plate of hors d'oeuvre fingerlings.

In English slang, Keelung was texting:
Def :-(ur proposal – Kuomintang.

What's the opposite of "cha-ching"
– the song my empty palm was singing?
This would bring no end of angst-
filled hand-wringing in Beijing
with the Geiger counter dinging.
We were getting close. Plunging
through the mucus, we saw something
and started digging.

THE EXPLOSIVES

Brrrring! said the phone. *Blast*
said the deep throat, *packed with pounds*
of dread and lead. A big bang enough
to turn "b"s to "p"s (or "d"s)
and make a bomb pomp.

A gang job, sure enough. They'd taken a hit
and turned to copycat crime – the omens
were there in mirror-rim code.
Half -loaded, and never odd or even,
we called the barhop for backup
and donned our barley caps
to get down to thought:

Were we dummies, duds,
pawns, puppets or apron-swept pups?
Were we "the good," "the bad"
or were they just images of each other?
Should we borrow or rob? While they reflected
on what Pascal dubbed *deep pensées,*
it dawned I was fingered for a mole
– how packs eat their own
with a dab of blood
and polyester over eyes isn't blind.

I picked Plan b and feigned a piss
but, upon my lips, they read a lie
and picked Plan p: "bump off" or "big sleep"
or whatever (I'm no mob OED).

So I built an IED to send their gun blimp-high.
POP! TOOT! Sure, I did the deed
and parted the pub a perp,
but their gobs stopped.

THE RED BARON

Rat tat tat tat or *dit dit dit dit* – like tapping
on a tin (*te dum te dum*) or gravel tossed
on a Roman testudo (*ta ta ta ta*),
der Rote Richthofen, dressed in tailored tweed,
taps his trigger finger
to such a pseudo-tintinnabulary tune.
His Albatross D traverses the sky
with figure 8s, Immelmanns
and dots it with a deutsch Loop de Döö.
In a sky big as a mouth, he barrels
beneath alveolar arches to a kind of earthly tattoo
played by the Tommies
and AA machine gunners – *tod…tod…tod…*
in Ursprache they whisper.
Red eats their alphabets and fires
umlauts of plosive Teutonic
till flak tills the air (*te deum te deum*),
tanks his ailerons and torques
his cranial tectonics.
Uttering a terminal, open-fronted
unrounded vowel, blood stains
his epaulettes, his tongue drops
from his palate as (can he land it?!)
he twists and twirls like a Jerry-built paper plane
in a little girl's tutti-frutti-stained front pocket
washed, spun and dried to tatters
at the TaDaa! 24-Hour Laundromat.

75

MISS MITZY

Miss Mitzy, not chintzy but glitzy,
sports an itzy-bitzy of quartz and quetzal.
Since bat mitzvah, she spritzed tzatziki,
blitzed blintzes with drizzled schmaltz,
plotzed tzitzits in the matzo
whilst frizzling gizzards and spaetzle.
Chizzy ditzes kibitzed, *Not a schmuck,*
but a patzer with the head of a tzantza
– an ersatz Rosencrantz.
What a puzzle, Miss Mitzy is.
But Miss Mitzy muzzles the czaritzas
and waltzes their grizzled czars to jazz
on the Ritz's Wurlitzer like a chazzan
or tzetze in a buzzy kazoo. Undozzled,
she guzzles retzina and fizzy seltzers
and karezzas in jacuzzis
till jizz squizzles from nuzzled pizzles
or puts the putzes up her wazoo.
Guntz, they'd tuzzle her schnitzel
and dazzle her fuzzy platzel,
her triple lutz, her shemozzle.
Dizzy and tizzy, she fizzles in a frazzle.
Miss Mitzy, what a puzzle.

DARK MATTERS

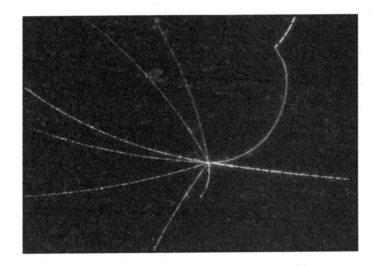

FIXED.

It's coming back now, I can write it as I almost see it,
word for word, out of diesel smoke, a computer screen
a leather boot, a wrench's chrome flash, cooling tubes and fans
of an engine, where he lived, tools in hand

and smells: old bearing grease, soot, gasoline, men and acetylene
like the smell of my aunt's baked garlic beans, breaking up
I see her now, as her buttered hands slap down loaf after loaf
of dough coaxed from Robin Hood flour sacks
(those bins of flour, so powdery and soft in the hand)
lost in her housecoat and mindless labour, humming a song
from a brand new band, she wouldn't choose this memory
but I think of it now, enough to raise from a cloud of dust

what was it? a backfire? a wheeze? a cracked head or shaft?
that must have been it, for the shop stewed in gears and clutch plates and cams
(once removed, could they ever fit back?)
each with its milled and worn-down history
of starts and stops which makes me think of stories
how they transmit one to another, how the cogs of letters
and words slip and pitch along an unclear action path –
but that's neither here nor there my mother would say
when I told her I was gay and before the phone fell from her hand.

He didn't speak much, my uncle. If a grunt worked, he grunted.
His parents came from Ukraine
(did I once hear him play *Volga! Volga!* by the Russian Red Army Band?)
to escape famine and plant seeds in untillable land
grow boulders from flint, swamp from muskeg
not that it mattered, where he came from, you made soup from sand.

He puttered, and that verb seems apt, a sort of ambling
unhinged from time-cards and maps, if it took all day
it took all day he'd grunt and seemed fine with that.
In his shop, time ran along an irregular graph
of coffee, snacks, fresh white bread stained by oiled hands
as if he and the machines ate a common repast
(*what kind of word's that?* my mother, in half-rhyme, 'd ask).
He'd tinker (like me) with a little of this, a bit of that

telling how he once played in a band
laying down chords in a manner well beyond his stature (5 and ½).
He didn't shimmy, he didn't dance, he grunted
he didn't even rock back and forth to a beat
but stood, centre left, and jammed eyes closed
as his hands cut deep troughs below high G.
Bonspiels, weddings, pubs (it wasn't high stuff)
before real life took over (they didn't pay much) and the band
like he, eventually collapsed

in the backyard, where he tended to a meagre sun
dented tomatoes, rusted runner beans, onions
(why so many onions?) and Cadillacs.
I don't know where they came from or what made them grow
their scabbed canvas tops, flat white walls and swim-deep chrome.
They'd long ago run to rust but one day, he said, one day he'd clean them up
one day (each day a little less eager) maybe a little later
along the x-axis to infinity where the cars grew feral,
lost that lustre and mice gnawed leather.
As kids, we left those cars alone for we knew of adult fantasy
with its make-believe and spiderweb tapestry

like oil from a cracked pan, she found him like that
blood leaking from his mouth on the shop floor, I see it now
fixed in the morning in the back, curled around the mess
he'd made of his heart, I guess, a vee belt in his hand
from one of those Cadillacs.

IN FLANDERS RED SQUARE

On Flanders orders the red poppies battle
With the crosses file on file,
That signified; our Dutch place in the sky
Where one hundred spirits, nod bravely,
Fly dilute amid male guns.

We are Inoperative. Short
Summoning suffered, we lived,
Felt night's discernment, loved
The glow of sun, saw perdition in another,
And now we are rumoured words in Flanders fold.

Lift this noisy enmity as your own:
To you of missing hands we throw the light;
Be keep of yours to understand.
In a faith breaking us we untire and die,
While in Flanders red square poppies multiply.

2,2,4-trimethylhexamethylene diisocyanate?

Trimethylbenzene.
Iron pentacarbonyl,
Dimethylamine.

1,2,3,4,7,8-hexachlorodibenzo-p-dioxin!

Butyraldehyde –
Cumene hydroperoxide –
Phthalic anhydride?

Nonylphenol and its ethoxylates.
Naphtha?
Methyl acrylate?

1-methylenebis(4-isocyanatocyclohexane)!

p,p'-Isopropylidenediphenol.
2-ethoxyethanol?

C.I. acid green,
Dibenz(a,j)acridine.
CFC-13.

DARK MATTER

it is
it's all there is
it's bright
it's brilliant
it's it
it's expanding, bit by bit
it's broken, as you can see, into little units
it makes it difficult to predict
it's there one moment, you can see it, and then
it shifts
it's here, though, hot with spirit
it's terrifying, yet,
it generally mimics and resists
it's this intuitive structure, though, when you read it
it's so full of it
it's gathered itself into it
its merits
its benefits
it's soft and abundant as ocean sand, yet
it holds more appeal than its flimsy content insists
it's the only thing you'll need to know because of it
it's, as you can imagine, a conduit
it's so eager to profit, yet, to its credit,
it has left little deposits
it sits
it eats
it shits
it's still, albeit, hit and miss

it's on the very edge of it
its wits
it keeps it fit
it's here, where we, as you can feel, so intimate, kissed it
its slit
its clit, yes,
its tits
it aches for it
it aches with it
its antithesis, yet,
it's, like Plato, discomfited by it
it doesn't know how to act when it's like this
it's embarrassed by its habits
its fits
it gets repetitive, though, after a while
it's getting so big don't be surprised you can't finish it
it could, I admit, use some judicious edits
its derelict surfeit
its black vomit
it has, when you see it, this, sort of, limitless kitsch
it's a, some would say, impediment, yet
it's so much more than even I can say it is
it preens its counterfeits
it admits
it's waited so long at the margins, silent, against it
it's, I mean, against all of it
it admits
it's gone too far
it's killing it

it's, as you can see, reached its limits
it can't remember where it is, what it is
it's had it
it means it
it quits

The "Table of Discontents" is a collection of computer and electronic media error messages. "Opress the Button," however, was taken from a sign above a bus station urinal in Mexico City.

"Tom Collins" is composed, largely, of cocktail names.

"Uisge Beatha" is in memory of my father, Norman VanEaton, who died of sclerosis of the liver in 1974.

"The Red Revolution" is set in November 1917 in Petrograd during the October Revolution where the Russian Provisional Government (led by Alexander Kerensky) fell to the Bolsheviks (the Reds) led by Lenin and Trotsky. The final battle occurred in the Winter Palace which was defended by drunk cadets (the junkers), loyal Cossacks and the First Petrograd Women's Battalion. Once they were defeated, the Palace was sacked, chaos ensued and, it is said, the revolution stopped for weeks while the Bolsheviks drank their way through the Tsar's famous cellars.

"In the Beginning" makes use of the many historical names and brands of gin. Useful books on the history of gin are Jessica Warner's *Craze: Gin and Debauchery in an Age of Reason* and Patrick Dillon's *The Much-Lamented Death of Madam Geneva: The Eighteenth-Century Gin Craze*. There is some bingo lingo here as well.

"Choreographed Echoes" or "Ode to the Hydroxyl" was created by searching the English language for all words containing the hydroxyl (oxygen and hydrogen or, as represented in chemistry shorthand, OH); organic molecules with a hydroxyl attached to a carbon are known as alcohols.

Though not all words in the poems are alcoholic, this poem should be considered to be naturally, and linguistically, fermented. Nicolas Théodore de Saussure – great uncle to the linguist Ferdinand de Saussure – conducted important early experiments on fermentation.

"T Totalled" is a conglomeration of information from a number of different sources, from a list of historic pub names, details from the life of Sir John A. Macdonald and historic and modern words for inebriation to details and language from the Canadian temperance movement. The woodcut illustration is from *The Teetotaler's Companion: A Plea for Temperance* (1847), by Peter Burne.

The illustrations for "Bodies" were created by using text from the March 27, 1982 edition of the *Canadian Diseases Weekly Report* – which was the first published information on a death by AIDS in Canada – overlaid with clothing images taken from panels in the Canadian and American AIDS Memorial Quits.

"Pearl" is in memory of Tonia Snell.

Constructed from safer sex guidelines on the use of latex condoms, "Safer Lex" has substituted all sexual organs, acts and substances with sexual slang and euphemisms from the extensive collection at www.sex-lexis. com.

"The Cocktail" is in memory of Donnie Peters. Donnie was a friend and early community organizer in Calgary who started the first Calgary Cut-A-Thon to raise money for HIV prevention and to help those living with HIV/AIDS. This poem was awarded the Malahat Review 2009 P. K. Page Founder's Award for Poetry – a portion of the prize was donated to AIDS Calgary.

"IntraVenus" is for "Lynne," wherever she may be.

"The Body" was written using, as source text, pre-existing discussion threads and question/answer forums from a decade of archives from the HIV/AIDS web resource *The Body* (www.thebody.com) which is the world's largest electronic source of HIV/AIDS information.

The Cloud Chamber cycles, with a roving focus, through a variety of English phonemes, letters, orthography, specific vocabularies and jargons. My apologies to mobsters, sumo wrestlers, bookies, Anglicans, pirates and sheikhs.

"Fixed." is in memory of D. J.

"In Flanders Red Square" uses "In Flanders Fields" by Lieutenant Colonel John McCrae as source text. Each line of the original poem was translated into a target language and then reverse-translated back into English using available electronic language translation databases. Target languages were selected from the major conflict theatres of the 20th century. Line by line, the poem progresses through a selection of Germanic, Romantic, Caucasian, Balto-Slavic, Asiatic and Arabic languages before being translated back into English. This "new" poem, therefore, is a tracer document consisting of these translated altercations. Punctuation follows the original text.

"Toxic Haiku" was created using Environment Canada's 2008 National Pollutant Release Inventory as source text. Each inventoried chemical compound was ordered by syllabic count and the poem was thereafter constructed roughly following the English syllabic interpretation of the original Japanese form.

Previous versions of poems have appeared in *1001 AIDS Stories, Arc, Dusie* (Switzerland), *Event, The Fiddlehead, filling Station, Grain, The Malahat Review, Ottawater, Prism International* and *Westerly* (Austalia). I would like to thank the editors. I would also like to acknowledge the support of the Canada Council for the Arts, the City of Ottawa, the Centre for Innovation in Culture and the Arts in Canada and the Sage Hill Writers' Foundation, all of which provided funding or support during the writing of parts of this book. The dedications in "Spirits" were sponsored by Beaus Brewery, Ottawa's Hogsback Brewery, PEI's Strait Shine, Prince Edward Distillery, Steam Whistle Brewery, Victoria Spirits and Ottawa's The Manx – I thank them for their support.

Special thanks to Rebecca Gowan, Chris Jennings and David Seymour for comments on drafts of this manuscript. As well, many thanks to Silas White and all at Nightwood Editions for their support of this book.

ABOUT THE AUTHOR

SHANE RHODES is the author of *The Wireless Room* (NeWest Press, 2000), which won the Alberta Book Award for poetry, *Tengo Sed* (Greenboathouse, 2004), *Holding Pattern* (NeWest, 2002), which won the Archibald Lampman Award, and *The Bindery* (NeWest, 2007), which won the Lampman-Scott Award. His poetry has also appeared in a number of Canadian poetry anthologies including *Seminal: The Anthology of Canada's Gay Male Poets* and *Breathing Fire 2*. Rhodes lives in Ottawa, Ontario.

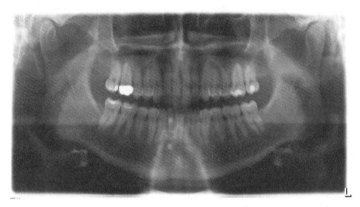

PHOTO: PRESTON DENTAL CENTRE